AF269747

Tough Tanks

Marie-Therese Miller

Lerner Publications ◆ Minneapolis

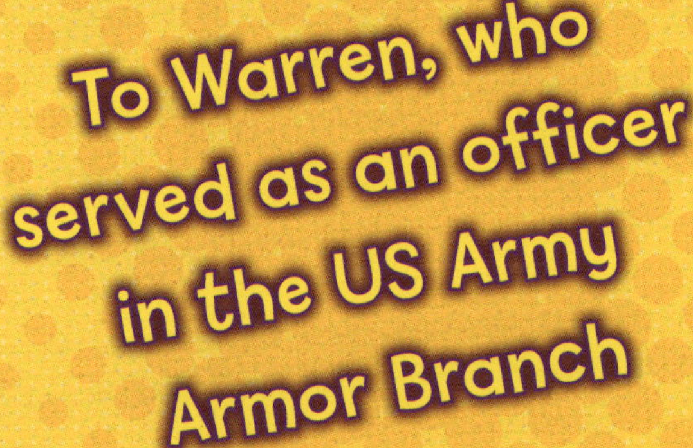

Lerner Publications Company
An imprint of Lerner Publishing Group, Inc.
241 First Avenue North
Minneapolis, MN 55401 USA

For reading levels and more information, look up this title at www.lernerbooks.com.

Main body text set in Billy Infant Regular. Typeface provided by SparkType.

Editor: Cole Nelson
Lerner team: Sue Marquis

Library of Congress Cataloging-in-Publication Data

Names: Miller, Marie-Therese, author.
Title: Tough tanks / Marie-Therese Miller.
Description: Minneapolis : Lerner Publications, [2025] | Series: Lightning bolt books : Mighty military vehicles | Includes bibliographical references and index. | Audience: Ages 6–9 | Audience: Grades 2-3 | Summary: "Tanks are big, strong, and can drive over almost anything in their way. How do such big vehicles move across the battlefield? Readers get a look inside tanks and learn what makes them so tough!"— Provided by publisher.
Identifiers: LCCN 2023041680 (print) | LCCN 2023041681 (ebook) | ISBN 9798765626160 (lib. bdg.) | ISBN 9798765629017 (pbk.) | ISBN 9798765635360 (epub)
Subjects: LCSH: M1 (Tank)—Juvenile literature. | Tanks (Military science)—United States—Juvenile literature.
Classification: LCC UG446.5 .M477 2025 (print) | LCC UG446.5 (ebook) | DDC 623.74/752—dc23/eng/20231006

LC record available at https://lccn.loc.gov/2023041680
LC ebook record available at https://lccn.loc.gov/2023041681

Manufactured in the United States of America
1-1009908-51950-11/16/2023

Table of Contents

M1 Abrams at Work

A tank rumbles across the field. Its tracks move easily from grass to sand to road.

Soldiers ride inside the tank. The loader places a round in the tank's main gun. The gun fires with a loud blast.

The US Army uses the M1 Abrams tank in combat.

These tanks are strong and tough.

Parts of a Tank

Abrams tanks move on tracks instead of tires. Tracks help them move across rough land.

These tanks are powered by a gas turbine engine. Heavy tanks need powerful engines to run.

The tank's turret has the
main gun, a cannon. Tanks
also have machine guns.

Tanks use grenade launchers to fire smoke grenades. **The smoke helps to hide the tank during battle.**

The driver sits in the driver's hole. The driver uses periscopes and cameras to see outside the tank.

A commander's hatch and a loader's hatch let people in and out of the turret. The commander comes out of a hatch to have a better view of the battlefield.

The loader uses a hatch to fire the machine gun. Loaders also load the cannon.

Inside the Tank

Each person in the tank has a role. Drivers drive the tank.

Gunners find a target. They fire the cannon. Gunners and loaders also fire machine guns.

The commander helps the gunner choose targets. They also use radios to share information with other tank commanders.

The commander sometimes fires one of the tank's machine guns.

The US military started using the M1 Abrams tank in 1980. New tanks have better sensors to find targets. They have stronger armor to protect the crew inside.

The US military has used tanks for over 100 years. The M4 Sherman was the main tank US troops used in World War II (1939–1945).

Tanks are mighty vehicles.
They are ready for battle, and they keep soldiers safe.

Vehicle Diagram

M1 Abrams

Fun Facts

- The first tanks were originally used in World War I (1914–1918).

- Tank crews can train on simulators and computers.

- The Abrams tank's turbine engine can run on jet fuel.

- Tanks have cameras that can detect heat to help find targets in the dark.

Glossary

armor: a protective outer covering on the tank

combat: fighting in a war

commander: the one in charge, especially in the military

hatch: a small door or opening

periscope: an instrument with mirrors and lenses that lets a person see around obstacles

round: a unit of ammunition

track: a belt fastened around the wheels of a heavy vehicle

Learn More

Britannica Kids: Tank
https://kids.britannica.com/students/article
/tank/277263

Hustad, Douglas. *US Army Equipment and Vehicles*.
Minneapolis: Kids Core, 2022.

Kiddle: Tank Facts for Kids
https://kids.kiddle.co/Tank

Miller, Marie-Therese. *Land and Water Combat
Vehicles*. Minneapolis: Lerner Publications, 2025.

National Geographic Kids: World War 1 Facts for Kids
https://www.natgeokids.com/uk/discover/history
/general-history/first-world-war/

Rossiter, Brienna. *Big Machines in the Military*. Lake
Elmo, MN: Focus Readers, 2021.

Index

Photo Acknowledgments

Image credits: SPC Kelsey M VanFleet/U.S. Army, p. 4; Sgt. Joaquin Vasquez-Duran/U.S. Army, p. 5; Cpl. Paul S. Martinez/U.S. Marine Corps, p. 6; Cpl. Alexander Sturdivant/U.S. Marine Corps, p. 7; Mark Schauer/U.S. Army, p. 8; Sgt. Alicia R. Leaders/U.S. Marine Corps, p. 9; Matthias Fruth/U.S. Army, p. 10; SSG Bill Boecker/U.S. Army National Guard, p. 11; Alex Kraus/Bloomberg via Getty Images, p. 12; Spc. Marcus Floyd/U.S. Army, p. 13; Cpl Gabrielle Quire/U.S. Marine Corps, p. 14; Spc. Juan Carlos Izquierdo/U.S. Army, p. 15; John Crosby/U.S. Army, p. 16; Sgt. James Dunn/U.S. Army, p. 17; Sgt. Major Corine Lombardo/U.S. Army National Guard, p. 18; p. 18; Markus Rauchenberger/U.S. Army, p. 19; Staff Sgt. Austin Berner/U.S. Army, p. 20.

Cover: SPC Kelsey M VanFleet/U.S. Army.